365 DAILY AFFIRMATIONS FOR CREATIVITY

365
DAILY AFFIRMATIONS FOR CREATIVITY

Janet Luongo

Hannacroix Creek Books, Inc.
Stamford, Connecticut

Copyright © 2005 by Janet Luongo
Cover art "Flourishings" by Janet Luongo, oil on canvas, 24x30 inches, 1984.

All rights reserved. No part of this book may be reproduced or transmitted in any form or by any means, electronic or mechanical, including photocopying, recording or by any information storage and retrieval system without written permission from the publisher, except for the inclusion of brief quotations in a review.

DISCLAIMER

The purpose of this book is to provide inspiration and opinions on the topic covered. It is sold with the understanding that neither the author nor the publisher are engaged in rendering artistic, creative, psychological, literary, or other professional services. Just as every person is unique, so too is everyone's creativity.

Typographical or content mistakes may inadvertently be contained in this book. The author and the publisher shall have neither liability nor responsibility to any person or entity with regard to any loss or damage caused, or alleged to be caused, directly or indirectly by the opinions or information contained in this book.

You may put a great deal of time and effort into reading this book and it still may not give you the results you wish. Neither this book nor its author or publisher in any way promise creativity or any other results.

Author's Acknowledgements:
My editor, Jan Yager; my husband, Jim Luongo; and my son, David.

Library of Congress Cataloging-in-Publication Data
Luongo, Janet, 1949-
365 daily affirmations for creativity / Janet Luongo.
p. cm.
Includes bibliographical references.
ISBN 1-889262-93-5
1. Creative ability--Miscellanea. 2. Affirmations. I. Title: Three hundred sixty-five daily affirmations for creativity. II. Title.
BF411.L46 2005
153.3'5--dc22
                                            2004022469

Published by:
Hannacroix Creek Books, Inc.
1127 High Ridge Road, #110 Stamford, CT 06905-1203 USA
Phone: 203-321-8674   Fax: 203-968-0193
www.hannacroixcreekbooks.com e-mail: hannacroix@aol.com

Contents

Foreword by Jack Canfield   vii
Introduction   1

Part 1: 365 Daily Affirmations for Creativity   15

1 I Believe I Am Original   17
2 I Draw on Inner Resources   21
3 Laughter, Music, and Dreams Spark My Creativity   25
4 I Seek Inspiration Everywhere   29
5 The Young Connect Me to My Imagination   34
6 I Understand the Creative Process   38
7 I Am Innovative at Work   43
8 I Am a Creative Leader   47
9 My Life is the Canvas Upon Which I Create   51
10 I Practice the Art of Relationships   56
11 My Passion is Unstoppable   60
12 My Spirit Continually Renews Me   65

Part 2: Exercises for Enhancing Creativity   71
　　For Individuals   73
　　Group Exercises   93

Part 3: Resources   111
　　Books and Articles   113
　　Websites   121
　　Associations   123

About the Author   125

365 Daily Affirmations for Creativity

Foreword
by
Jack Canfield

How many times do you look for the answers to your problems outside yourself? *365 Daily Affirmations for Creativity* starts off by pointing you in the right direction—the answer lies within. If you want to be more creative in your personal and professional life, positive beliefs about yourself and drawing on inner resources are essential.

You have to take full responsibility for everything you experience in your life. You have control over just three things —the thoughts you think, the images you visualize, and the actions you take. Doing these three things in a positive frame of mind determines the life experiences you will have. This book on affirmations helps you to find the words for positive thoughts, and helps you to envision positive images. The excellent exercises for creativity then lead you to take specific actions.

Creative thinking is essential in the 21st century. Flexibility and open-mindedness are critical to moving forward. If required, you have to take a new action. If you keep doing what you've always done, you'll keep getting what you've always gotten. If you want something different, you're going to have to do something different!

While this compact book will provide the inspiration and guidance in being more creative, you are the one who will execute the strategies and incorporate the principles into your everyday life. Reading and repeating a daily affirmation will start a good daily habit. Simply stated, a habit is something you do so often it becomes easy. In other words, it's a behavior that you keep repeating. If you persist at developing a new behavior, eventually it becomes automatic.

There's no such thing as a magic "quick-fix" formula. It takes real commitment to create positive transformation. It's in your hands to create the life you want. This small book fits easily in your hands and pocket, but don't just read it once. Read an affirmation every day until you absorb its wisdom.

Affirm yourself, visualize accomplishments, and most of all, take daily action. May your life be truly enriched in the process.

Jack Canfield is co-author of the *Chicken Soup for the Soul®* book series and co-author of *The Success Principles: How to Get From Where You Are to Where You Want to Be*.

Introduction

The imagination ignites progress in every area of our civilization. With society changing at a mind-boggling rate, we all need to develop our creative capacity to its maximum to face the current and future challenges.

I have spent my entire career as an artist and educator researching the conditions in schools and workplaces to learn how to induce a creative state of mind that produces the best innovative ideas. Whether you are a student, teacher, entrepreneur, artist, writer, scientist, professional, manager, employee, leader or change agent, in order to go forward, you need words of encouragement. If you are not hearing positive words from the people around you, you must say them to yourself. Earl Nightingale, who established an industry based on positive thinking, popularized ancient Sanskrit wisdom by stating simply, "You become what you think about."

Affirmations are positive statements expressed in the present tense. These statements do not identify something you will do, could do, or will try to do. Instead, affirmations express the simple truth of your being as it exists right *now*. The rich literature on the power of affirmations to transform lives can be found in the work of many thinkers, such as Jack Canfield, Carolyn Myss, Dr. Phil McGraw, Shakti Gawain, and Eckhart Tolle.

I've been asked why I wrote this book of affirmations on creativity. The answer is that early in my life I chose to affirm, not to denigrate, myself as an artist and it has made all the difference. In grade school, one of my teachers inspired me when she told me I had artistic gifts and a light to share. Believing in that light has lightened up my path.

Creativity is part of our natural inheritance; it needs to be exercised as much as our bodies and minds. Affirmations are one way to exercise and enhance our creativity. It is one of the proven methods, including experiencing the arts, that allow us to enter more imaginative states of mind.

I have learned that humor is also essential to open-mindedness. In childhood, my best friend's witty observations and jokes, which made me laugh so hard I fell down, caused me to see things differently—an important stimulant for creativity. When I was sixteen, my first job was as an assistant to a black mural painter in New York City; I learned from his struggles the necessity of having a rock-solid belief in one's originality.

A crisis early in my life taught me the most. After a confusing family break-up, I left home much too young and tackled living on my own in New York City, trying all the while to stay in art school. A poor choice to try a psychedelic drug led me to fall apart while still a teen. While my father told me that doctors said I might not ever lead a "normal life" (code for having a husband, children and a job), and that I should forget about college, there was something deep inside me that didn't accept that dismal prognosis.

I recalled the words of my childhood teacher who believed I had gifts to share and I pictured again my childhood dreams of a full and happy future. With my mother's help I returned to college and eventually earned a master's degree. I fell in love with a wonderful man who became my life partner; together we've raised our beautiful son who just graduated from college.

Nourished by all the creative spirits who influenced me, I help people develop words and pictures in their minds that are full-color images of the best they have to give. I have compiled the philosophy I developed in the form of short affirmations so that even the most rushed person can find a way to start the day right. I know this guidance would have helped me through my dark times. I hope the words in this book will help you as you struggle to make your voice audible, your soul visible, or your ideas public.

I have been fortunate to have a fulfilling career that spans many aspects of the arts. My confidence restored, when I later moved to Switzerland, I set out to fulfill my childhood dream of becoming an artist and showing my work in Paris. After several rejections, a gallery finally accepted my paintings. I never imagined transporting my works to Paris would become an ordeal. But I never gave up despite bureaucratic obstacles, losing my wallet, getting lost, and running out of gas. I still succeeded in getting my paintings to the exposition!

I wrote this book because I want to share the value of a creative approach that helps me in all areas of my life. The avoidance of stereotyped roles has allowed my husband, son, and me to create a lifestyle that supports the family unit as well as each of us as individuals. Yoga, meditation, and dream study teaches me to tune in to my inner voice. Writing journals and novels helps me make sense of personalities and events. Painting moves me out of verbal, logical and linear thinking into the realm of the holistic and spiritual.

To bring out the gifts of each individual, I speak and conduct workshops in educational, cultural, and spiritual centers in the United States, Canada and Europe. To fulfill the mission of my company, I apply the skills I gain from the arts to becoming a stronger leader and entrepreneur. People in the workplace—from researchers to supervisors and CEOs—who practice positive affirmations are more focused, successful, and accomplished.

From my travels and reading, I find similarities between the approaches of innovative people from diverse cultures and from seemingly opposite fields. As an executive at a museum of art and science, I discovered scientists and inventors who are as wildly creative as any artist, writer, or musician.

I've been greatly enriched by conversations with people and studies of monuments and art on four continents. As a painter and teacher living in Europe for eight years, I worked with children, teachers and parents from dozens of world cultures. I was inspired, like the French impressionists, by the contemplative art of China and Japan as well as by painters such as surrealist Frida Kahlo, who was partly Hungarian, like me, but celebrated in her dress her Mexican heritage. I identify with her courage in overcoming the deep wounds she experienced as a girl.

In exploring the lives of creative people, I find many who triumphed over crippling conditions. The determined attitude of these brave people is encouraging. It is well-known that the great Dutch post-impressionist Vincent van Gogh was rejected from art school and never sold a painting in his lifetime, yet he is now world renowned with the price of his art breaking records.

Less well known are women artists such as Artemesia Gentileschi, who could only obtain art materials through her father, an artist, was victimized by her tutor, but went on to become a greatly admired painter of the Italian Baroque.

As recounted in her autobiography, *I Know Why the Caged Bird Sings*, Maya Angelou, who was raised poor, was so traumatized during her childhood by a sexual assault that she would not speak for years. She conquered her fears and was selected to read her poetry at the Presidential Inauguration of Bill Clinton.

Galileo was put under house arrest for his revolutionary theory that the planets revolve around the sun.

What helps visionary people through the gauntlet of adversity, assault, criticism, mockery and discrimination? Often it is a simple belief in themselves, their purpose, and the power of their ideas.

Research to support the effectiveness of visualization is mounting in the high-stakes arena of sports. Beyond numerous anecdotal accounts of many athletes such as golfing great Jack Nicklaus, who said he "watched a movie" in his head before each shot, the scientific data is impressive. In an experiment described by Dr. Judd Blaslotto, basketball players were randomly assigned to experimental groups at the University of Chicago. They were tested and then retested after thirty days on their free-throw proficiency. In Jaime T. Licauco's report in *Asia Africa Intelligence Wire* in 2003, he quotes Dr. Blaslotto: "The players who hadn't practiced at all showed no improvement" or "exhibited a drop. Those who had physically practiced one hour each day showed a performance increase of 24 percent. Here's the clincher: the visualization group, by merely imagining themselves successfully shooting free throws, improved 23 percent!"

Other researchers confirm these findings. In "The mind of a champion" in *Natural Health Magazine* in 1997, Phil Scott quotes Robert Schleser, director of the Institute for Sport and Performance Psychology at the Illinois Institute of Technology, who had been studying the effects of imagery for twenty years. "We know this works because it's been proven—and it's quantified." Scott also refers to a study of golf students by Shane Murphy, former chief sports psychologist for the U.S. Olympic Committee. Scott reports Murphy's results: "Over a six-day period, the third who were told to visualize themselves making a perfect putt improved their scores by 30 percent; the third who were told to not visualize anything improved by 10 percent; and the third who were told to imagine barely missing the putt grew worse by 21 percent. The lesson is that everything you tell yourself while visualizing must be phrased positively."

Coach Jim Johnson used tapes of affirmations to instill positive mental attitudes that make champions. In her article, "In my mind I'm going to be a star," published in *U.S. News and World*

Report in 1987, Lynn Rosellini reports that Johnson believed mentally rehearsing perfect hits can help make them happen. His case in point was a baseball player who had mediocre ability but because of mental toughness he broke records in hitting. The player's name was Pete Rose.

Although recent data emanates from sports psychology, the effects ripple through many other areas. Artists, who have relied on forms of affirmation and visualization for millennia, feel validated by the new research. Jane Magrath, professor and director of piano pedagogy at the University of Oklahoma in Norman, writes that in terms of performance, "a student might be helped by visualizing the way it feels, both emotionally and physically, to play a piece well in a performance." Researchers on science learning, Lauren Cifuentes and Yi-Chuan Jane Hsieh, found that visualization as a study strategy led to students' improved test performances. America's great philosopher of education of the early 20th century, John Dewey, believed images were essential to learning.

Considering all the research, it is best practice to read a chosen affirmation, repeat it out loud several times, and at the same time visualize an accompanying image, imagining with all the senses something positive actually taking place.

I have personally worked hard to become aware of how the subconscious dwells on fears, anxieties, regrets, doubts, judgments, and worries. As soon as I "hear" myself thinking useless, draining thoughts that suck the life out of me, I stop. I focus on the present, my breathing, immediate sights and sounds, the gifts I'm grateful for, things I do well, and people I can help. I listen to uplifting music or tapes. It works! I feel the energy return as I repeat positive statements to myself, and good people and things are attracted to my life.

How can you use this book? Like the months of the year, the affirmations are organized thematically into twelve sections. You may read this little book all at once, you may read one theme at a time, or just one affirmation a day over a year. After one month of daily practice, you will hopefully be on your way to new, positive habits of mind. Take a moment to absorb, reflect and visualize after you read each affirmation. Highlight the affirmations that speak to you the most; you may return to them as needed to sustain hope. You are invited to write your own affirmations in the back. The book is compact enough to keep with you.

Each of the twelve sections is based on one of my core beliefs that have guided me on my own journey to a positive and creative life. I live by the following:

I Believe I Am Original. In research by Fred Pryor of Career Track on the characteristics of creative people, it was found that it is not talent, genius, or particular circumstances that lead people to create. The single most important determinant is simply the belief that they are creative.

I Draw on Inner Resources. The second trait that most creative people share is that they pay attention to their inner lives from which they gain their unique perspectives that bring so much to the world.

Laughter, Music, and Dreams Spark My Creativity. The wisest people don't take themselves too seriously. On the other hand, small-minded people often say they are "dead" serious, and deadening they are. Music has the power to transform our energy and jar memories. Like humor and music, dreams transport us to different states of mind.

I Seek Inspiration Everywhere. Cross-fertilization of ideas leads to new creations. Forests and friends, fun and films spark the creative imagination.

The Young Connect Me to My Imagination. Children inspire adults with their unabashed curiosity and fresh creations. Many artists, like Picasso and Matisse, sought to see with the eyes of a child.

I Understand the Creative Process. Creative people, across just about every field, work in similar ways. Most creative people are aware of the process that goes something like this: detect a problem, mull it over, experience the "aha," experiment and produce, and then step back and evaluate.

I Am Innovative at Work. In the workplace, it is usually those who come up with lots of ideas who are perceived as being creative. However, generating ideas is not the end of the creative process, just like birthing a child is not the end of parenting. Everyone can contribute his or her skills to the process.

I Am A Creative Leader. Leaders are a lot like artists. They start with a passion. They need to have vision and to communicate so that others see the same big picture. They often see things others do not see and create original products and services. They need to be flexible and creative enough to change course on a dime. They take risks, embrace change, have the discipline to persevere, and create teams that harmonize like a fine-tuned orchestra.

My Life is the Canvas Upon Which I Create. Creativity can be applied to all problems that are encountered at home, at school, and at work. It becomes a habit of mind to consider all aspects of a situation, to reconsider tradition, and ask if there is a better way.

I Practice the Art of Relationships. Families and relationships are changing so rapidly it is essential to be flexible with the people with whom we are involved.

My Passion is Unstoppable. Once you know what you love, watch out!

My Spirit Continually Renews Me. When you create, you are aligning yourself with the mystery of all that is created. Both creative and spiritual impulses are satisfied when you stop in daily life to observe, admire, quietly reflect, and stand in awe at the magnificence of the world, the mind's power to interpret it, and the spirit's impulse to express it.

The second part of the book consists of sixty exercises to provide additional stimulation for your creativity. The first set of thirty exercises is for you to do on your own. The second set of thirty exercises is for teachers, trainers, and managers to use whether at school, work or on retreat, and may also be used by individuals. People of all ages and from all walks of life in Canada, Switzerland, and many states of the United States who participated in my Creativity Workouts have reported being energized by these exercises.

The third part of this book consists of resources on creativity including books and articles, as well as websites and associations that you might find useful.

It is my hope that from the daily affirmations, the exercises and the resources, you will find something that will inspire and stimulate your creativity and will lead you to a more prosperous and fulfilling life. Please write to me about how this book is helping you.

Ultimately, creativity is not about *having* anything. It is primarily about *being* who you are. Then it is about *doing.* Simply have the courage to start, in some small way, every day, doing the things you love. There is no single way to be creative. There is no one lifestyle. Artists have been hermits and socialites, rich and poor, modest and flamboyant. You just need to let go, get out of your own way, and let the gorgeous, unique soul within you fearlessly shine its bright light for all the world to see.

Janet Luongo
Artist and speaker on creativity and leadership
Open Minds Open Doors, LLC
Norwalk, Connecticut
www.openminds-opendoors.com
janet@openminds-opendoors.com

Part 1

365 Daily Affirmations

for Creativity

365 Daily Affirmations for Creativity

1

I Believe I Am Original

1. I believe in myself as a creative person.

2. Creativity is the very essence of what makes us human since the dawn of our history.

3. I reflect upon my "origin," the root of the word *original*.

4. The more original I am, the less I can be duplicated and the more valuable my contribution.

5. My creative act is the best way I know to uphold my right to freedom of expression.

6. I was given the gifts that I have in order to bring them out into the world, not to hide them.

7. The way to start a new work of art is to begin.

8. I am a unique individual and no one sees things exactly as I do.

9. I bring my creative spirit to every aspect of my life—work and play, professional and personal.

10. Just as no one on Earth has my same fingerprints or DNA, so no one else can create what I do in the same way.

11. Within me flows an infinite source of original ideas. Others are advised not to imitate but to draw from their own wells.

12. I am not afraid to be a solitary voice saying the truth of what I see. Others may either see it but don't say it, or may see it after I say it.

13. Though I don't always know where my creative drive will take me, I trust the work to be the vehicle that leads the way.

14. I revel in my natural abilities—I do not hide them, deny them or take them for granted. Nor do I think they make me superior in any way.

15. I have more fun and arrive at creative insights faster when I travel in twists and turns than when I move in a boring straight line.

16. I usually do not think in sequence. I advance, leaping from one point to another, and may return later to fill in a gap, if needed.

17. My creative mind resists dogma and thinking in absolute black and white terms.

18. Engaging with art makes me a fuller human being.

19. I create, not only because I *want* to, but because I *need* to and therefore I overcome all sorts of unfavorable conditions.

20. I declare myself a creative person who has the right to time and space and resources. This takes courage.

21. I am taking action today on my desire to create something.

22. I am working regularly and steadily on the art that I love.

23. I affirm my own style, clarifying rather than compromising it.

24. I concentrate on the thing that only I, with my special gifts, can do. Let the things other people can do…be done by other people!

25. My creative spirit is like the fragile golden leaf that shivers in the autumn wind, yet is so strong it hangs on all winter.

26. The contemplation of breath-taking beauty spurs my creative urges. I surround myself with beautiful things so that I am inspired.

27. Although my creativity involves solitude I am not lonely because I am filled with the luminous presence of great people and ideas.

28. While attempting to *master* an art form, I start with *loving* it. Mastery follows love.

29. If I choose to share my work, I know it is worthy of an audience.

30. The first step in the act of creation is to know who I am and what my message is.

2

I Draw on Inner Resources

31. One of the most important things I do to be creative is cultivate my inner life.

32. As if my mind were a radio, I am tuning out static and complaints, and tuning in trumpets and cheers.

33. I create because it's natural to me. When Picasso was asked why he paints, he answered, "Why do birds sing?"

34. My personal inner joy and sorrow is the soil from which will grow the fruit and flowers of my creations.

35. I keep the pipeline open to my emotions and thoughts, the fuel for my creative engine.

36. The richer and deeper a creator's inner life, the more original her or his creations.

37. I am enjoying fantasies that lift me out of mundane reality and stimulate my imagination.

38. Before I can create work about anyone or anything else, I develop awareness of myself.

39. Deep down within me I find motivations and urges to create that are unique to myself and that will produce work unlike that of any others.

40. I enjoy spending time in solitude and silence, just allowing myself to be fully aware of the present moment.

41. I value my own intuition, as did one of the great mathematicians of the 19th century, Henri Poincare, who believed we need intuition to make discoveries.

42. My primary work is discovering my unique point of view; the techniques I need for mastery are secondary and will follow.

43. In persevering in pursuit of my creative dream, I am pulling on inner resources I never knew existed.

44. I marvel at the mystery of how inspiration flows through me once I am in the act of creation.

45. All the answers I need lie within me.

46. A laudable goal of an artist is not to be known, but to know.

47. For a change, I think *inside* the box, exploring my own thoughts.

48. I am stilling my mind, which is like a placid lake, by damming the flood of turbulent thoughts.

49. When I must use my *head,* my intellect may be useful, but for creativity I also fully involve my *heart* and *body.*

50. I enjoy simply being myself, not acting out a fantasy or stereotype of "the artist."

51. I am living a creative life by living my own true life.

52. I am liberated from ever having to fill a role that doesn't ring true to my creative identity.

53. In the rush of creative ideas, I am gladly flushing negative thoughts out of my system.

54. I am patient and do not force my creativity into a pre-determined mold.

55. I get a thrill from using my imagination.

56. I don't use drugs or alcohol to falsely jumpstart creativity; my buoyant energies give me a natural feeling of joy.

57. I am the gardener of my own soul, nurturing the miraculous growth of the seedlings within me.

58. I am calling on my intuition to guide me when I have a gut feeling that a certain action is right for me.

59. I am listening to the murmurs of my heart, which whispers deep truths.

60. I am enjoying the cycle of my creative life, which alternates between being and doing.

3

Laughter, Music, and Dreaming Spark My Creativity

61. Both humor and creativity allow me to see the funny side of a difficult situation, freeing me to act in new ways.

62. Creative people, like humorists, combine odd elements to help us see things differently.

63. Today I am taking nothing seriously; I begin my creative work with cartoons, stand-up comics, clips of funny movies, and humorous recordings.

64. I am donning a funky hat, tee-shirt or costume, just for the fun of it.

65. When I laugh hard I forget my role and what I'm "supposed" to do, and suddenly there I am—an individual in all my unmasked splendor.

66. A dream is a wake-up call to what I need to pay attention to in my life and creative work.

67. I don't rush to jump out of bed in the morning since I receive some of my best insights in the moments between sleep and wakefulness.

68. I do simple drawings from dreams using basic colors, shapes, and symbols; these images help me understand my dream in a non-verbal way.

69. I am keeping a journal of my dreams because the unusual events and sequences that occur in dreams can be the key to a creative problem that occupies me.

70. I value the state of mind that occurs during dreaming because the slow brain waves, theta, are fertile ground for generating intuitive solutions.

71. My dreams help me approach issues differently: sometimes I float above them, sometimes I see them upside down, sideways and backwards.

72. I am tapping into deep sources of awareness by visualizing images, which is the language of the unconscious according to the psychologist Carl Jung.

73. Although I am serious about my creative endeavor, at times I let go and laugh at myself.

74. To stimulate my brain's creativity, I use art, metaphor, symbols, emotions, and play.

75. I am listening to classical music, which stimulates the neurons in my brain to be receptive to complex organization.

76. In playing a game, I am moving, singing, listening, and observing all at once, which is not only fun but is charging up my brain.

77. When I move differently, I think differently.

78. I listen to different kinds of music to trigger a variety of rich associations.

79. When I need to "pump up" my creative spirit I listen to the dance music of Aretha Franklin; when I need to go inward, I listen to classical Mozart.

80. I am in a state of reverie from a concert of music by Debussy.

81. To release inhibitions and to get my team laughing, I am giving out awards for the most outrageous ideas.

82. I celebrate my emotions and senses not as "icing on the cake," but as primary ingredients needed in any creative recipe.

83. I am doing common things in uncommon ways, which is fun and energizes me.

84. The easy rhythm of walking, the regular tapping of foot to earth, is drumming away cloudy thinking.

85. I am making visible and audible concepts that are invisible and silent.

86. I enjoy reverie so my brain waves, like ocean waves, roll calmly, and creative ideas, like gulls, dive in and take a ride.

87. I am creating art that expands the sense of the way the world might be, and possibilities of who I might be.

88. I am doing everything I can to loosen up. When I *drop* an inhibition, I usually *pick up* a good idea or two.

89. Rather than feel anger at human flaws, which closes me down, I laugh at human folly, which opens me up.

90. I am free to be outlandishly creative.

4

I Seek Inspiration Everywhere

91. I gather raw material for creativity from everyone I meet, from everyday sounds I hear, and from images that are everywhere to be found.

92. I am continuously inspired by the beauty in nature—a cat purring, an orchid's beard, the startling red of a cardinal.

93. I look at everything, as did Leonardo da Vinci, from at least three perspectives to stimulate my creative thinking.

94. I spend time closely observing an "image"—the root of the word *imagination*.

95. I am stimulated by the ideas of other creators and take time to read literature, listen to music and watch beautiful films.

96. I am changing something in my surroundings—a picture, screen saver, wall color or plant—that makes my approach to my creative work different, too.

97. Observing the extraordinary designs of nature, I clear my head of ordinary human constructs.

98. I am combining two ordinary things that were never connected before, thus creating something new and extraordinary.

99. To develop the capacity for logic needed to solve problems creatively, I am doing a puzzle, cracking a mathematical problem, or learning a foreign language.

100. To find inventive ideas, I look everywhere, like the writer Virginia Woolf, whose sources included Shakespeare, the classics of history, and insects.

101. My own courage is fortified as I read about creative people who stood fast and stayed true to their visions.

102. I am posting a picture or quote from a person who serves as a creative role model for me.

103. I am surrounding myself with a group of supportive people who advise me and encourage me to be courageous with my creative talents.

104. In my experiments I welcome serendipity—unexpected findings that lead me to new discoveries.

105. I am intensely observant to details and keenly alert to nuance, which brings subtlety to my work.

106. My intensity is attracting people and opportunities that will lead to further creative development.

107. In the quest for new knowledge in science and other fields, new information is continually renewing my views of the world.

108. I welcome the irrelevant and irreverent, provocative and intrusive—all of which jolt me into new thinking.

109. To get off old tracks of thinking, I am exploring an exhibit or jewelry store, where I wander down new paths of the imagination.

110. I am buoyed by the knowledge of all the things that are now possible—like flight, medical cures and wireless communication—which were once declared impossible.

111. I am going on a brief adventure to someplace new—a harbor, a park, a new neighborhood—which opens up new perceptions.

112. Interacting with people from different cultures makes me think about my everyday life in totally new ways.

113. I look at favorite images that relax and center me, that make me feel like myself—sensitive, warm, and funny.

114. I appreciate with new eyes something I encounter every day—a flowering bush, a picture, and a store clerk—but will never take for granted again.

115. In unexpected places I find out curious things—I learn history at the baseball stadium, storytelling at the senior center, and sociology at the park.

116. I am making notes and sketches from the designs of others, but am interpreting to create something of my own.

117. To find solutions I am reaching across artistic disciplines, like the poet Blake who painted watercolors, and the sculptor Michelangelo who penned sonnets.

118. I spend time in the company of creative people from all fields—from artists to inventors—to learn from their approaches to work and life.

119. I travel and absorb "foreign" ideas because many flourishings of creativity, such as the Renaissance, arose from the cross-pollination of ideas.

120. As a creator I connect fields considered opposites, like the composer Stravinsky who believed his thought process was similar to that of a mathematician.

5

The Young Connect Me to My Imagination

121. I am looking at life as if I were a child, as artists Henri Matisse and Paul Klee did, to see the startling newness of everything.

122. Like an uninhibited child, I dare to sing, paint and dance to express my own feelings.

123. My memories of what I loved as a child are giving me ideas for what I am creating today.

124. Looking at children's books and illustrations, I am recalling my own creative childhood and I am freely making associations.

125. I am cherishing the fresh views of children and especially admire their curiosity, enthusiasm, and ready laughter.

126. I am remembering myself as the child under five who was wildly creative and had more questions than answers.

127. I take care to nurture the creativity in all children I encounter.

128. I am enjoying being with children because they have no deadening pre-conceived notions.

129. I am spending some time at play, like children do, to rekindle my spirit of wonder and delight.

130. For this moment I am letting go of my traditional adult perspective of responsibility, which may hinder creativity.

131. I am embracing the child's attitude, "I can do it!"

132. I am recalling the things I loved to do and had wondered about when I was a child, which were the beginnings of life-long passions.

133. The spontaneity of children continues to challenge me to be as original as they are.

134. We each have a unique story to tell, in our own way, in our own time.

135. I find fresh ways of saying things, avoiding as much as possible the use of labels and clichés.

136. I am going back in time to revisit those early influences that set me on my path to creativity.

137. In cultivating the talents and values of the children in my life, I am creating the future.

138. I am wary of expert views that are more rigid and narrow than those of curious amateurs or children.

139. I make time to allow children to absorb and demonstrate understanding of new knowledge.

140. I provide many sensory experiences with art materials so children may absorb and retain concepts.

141. I celebrate the originality of children and reward those who find an unusual way to approach a challenge.

142. I am delighted when I find that there are numerous non-identical solutions to an artistic problem I posed.

143. Whenever possible, I allow children a choice—of materials, colors, approaches, or topics—so they "own" their creations.

144. When I praise a child's creations, I give my honest reaction and give specifics of what I like.

145. I ask a child to tell me about his creation, rather than tell him what I see or what it should be or how it should look.

146. I overcome fear of failure by informing students that their creative associations and responses, unlike facts or numbers, cannot be right or wrong.

147. Each person is as unique as a snowflake—there is a basic pattern but no two have ever been found to be exactly alike.

148. Teachers and techniques come into our lives as we need them, after we know what we want to create.

149. I open up possibilities for children to express their intelligences and talents, though I myself may lack expertise in that area.

150. It is every person's birthright to reach his or her full creative potential.

6

I Understand the Creative Process

Stage One: I cultivate my creative idea

151. I see that something could be done differently; becoming aware of a problem is what motivates many painters, poets, writers, and physicists to create.

152. I am making note of the odd thing that doesn't fit, the defect that needs correction, and am defining the problem that needs fixing.

153. I am reviewing all the elements that are working, and exploring what might be needed to make it all work better.

154. I am generating as many different alternatives as possible, even though I may return to the first option.

155. At the beginning stage of my creative work, I am letting my ideas flow uncorrected, unstructured and unjudged.

156. I am keeping a sketchbook for visual ideas because they are a real stimulus to all kinds of creativity.

157. In order to think *outside* the box, I am revisiting the box itself—structure is a starting point. Constraints can kick off creativity.

158. I respect the point of view of others, even though I may not agree with them, because they help me to see the whole picture.

159. I do original research and conduct fresh interviews to find new knowledge that I integrate with my own experience.

160. I read widely outside my field, mining books and magazines for ideas to apply to my own work.

161. Rather than force my thoughts to converge on one correct answer, I allow them to diverge in a variety of fascinating directions.

162. I am considering a *useless* idea and finding it very *useful*, in fact, because it demonstrates what does not work.

163. A seemingly crazy idea can spark a great idea.

164. I steep myself in the tools and ideas of my creative field so that I am highly equipped to launch new ideas.

Stage Two: I allow my ideas to incubate

165. One of the first things I do to enter new dimensions of thinking or feeling is to…slow…down….

166. I am letting go of all the hard work I have put into my project and am allowing my subconscious mind to let something new take shape.

167. I am taking the time to walk, shower, drive, daydream, play, catnap, or relax in some way so that my creative ideas can incubate.

168. I exercise regularly and find that when my body is energized, a flow of ideas is generated.

169. I am accepting the idle times, knowing that deep quiet and relaxation are necessary to prepare for the next surge in creative activity.

Stage Three: I am inspired

170. I have a startling clear vision of what I want to create.

171. I pay attention to my gut feelings because, as Einstein knew, they are important to productive thought.

172. I am actively capturing and documenting the flashes of insights because they are precious and fleeting.

Stage Four: I act on my idea

173. I enjoy as part of the creative process the gathering of data and facts that support my hypothesis or are needed for my literary or visual art.

174. I am keeping the appointment I made with myself to do creative work as faithfully as I would an appointment with an employer, client, doctor or friend.

175. I am putting one small mark down on a blank page. This act helps me begin what seems a daunting project—a finished work of art.

176. Many concrete ideas come to me in the "doing" stage, which could not have arrived in the abstract conceiving stage.

177. I commit, no matter what, to spending at least fifteen minutes a day on my creativity. (Before I know it, I'm involved for longer periods!)

178. I work hard with the tools of my craft and spend long hours preparing so that, in the end, ironically, my result will appear obvious and spontaneous.

Stage Five: I step back and check it out

179. I maintain a flexible frame of mind as I construct my interpretation of reality. As new pieces of information appear, I expand my frame.

180. I am stepping back to evaluate in the last stage of the creative cycle, and begin once again to question how I can do things differently.

7

I Am Innovative at Work

181. I apply to my work the traits that the arts develop—self-knowledge, concentration, observation, self-discipline, sensitivity, and teamwork.

182. Creativity means putting something new in the world, and I am doing that every day.

183. I am creating whenever I put people or events together that were never arranged that way before.

184. Through my creative impulses I embrace diversity. For both creativity and diversity, I need to consider multiple perspectives.

185. My reputation and image as a creative person is built up by a series of clever and unusual moves.

186. When I need to get the attention of people I avoid the boring, mechanical, and pedantic and become entertaining, colorful and novel.

187. I am more successful being unpredictable and remembered than by being boring and forgotten.

188. I think of creative ways of using bright color, odd stamps, funny cartoons, and witty quotes to make my message stand out.

189. I am cultivating my own creative style in everything from clothing and belongings to the way I greet and interact with people.

190. My creativity makes me stand out from the pack. I don't do what the rest of the crowd is doing—I deliberately go the other way.

191. In brainstorming, the first step in the innovation process, there is no room for judgment, criticism or perfectionism.

192. I am hosting a "Failure Fest" to laugh with others about the worst ideas we ever had and how we lived to tell the tale. Booby prizes are awarded.

193. Like cleaning out a drain, I am discarding layer after layer of assumptions and constraints that have held up my creative flow.

194. I don't *resist* change but actively *embrace* change.

195. I am switching responsibilities with someone at work today and then comparing notes on how we might do our jobs differently.

196. I put together teams that are diverse in all ways—style, age, gender, race, position, background, belief system, and area of expertise—to stimulate creative exchange.

197. When I "break down" in laughter, old mental structures also come apart, ready to be put back together again in new ways.

198. While working on something creative, I periodically rest my mind to allow something new and refreshing to emerge.

199. Whatever my personal style or skills, I am playing a role in innovation.

200. I am building on what others have done, standing on the shoulders of giants, or passing the ball in a relay race.

201. I am spontaneous and flexible, finding clever ways to get around roadblocks.

202. I am thinking BIG!

203. I see and clearly define problems that need to be solved and improvements that can be made.

204. I energize and motivate others to take unconventional steps.

205. I sense the essence in complex situations.

206. I take time to understand what works and what doesn't work so I can readjust my creative efforts.

207. I am using my skills in improvisation to think on my feet when unexpected situations arise.

208. I am giving up on small incremental changes that just prolong dysfunction and am overhauling the entire system.

209. I propose rewriting rules that are no longer useful.

210. Even where things seem adequate, I continue to look for ways to do things with less time, money, and effort—and with more fun!

8

I Am A Creative Leader

211. I am developing an imagination that senses what the future may bring, and am often considered ahead of my time.

212. I know that my creative ideas and knowledge, as well as those of my co-workers, are the most valuable capital of my company.

213. I am creating an environment that will attract the most creative, passionate, and reliable people.

214. To encourage creativity, I set up spaces for informal interaction, I create beautiful natural rest areas, and I am open to dialogue.

215. I am transforming my company culture to encourage people to be accountable and to be free to make decisions about their jobs.

216. I am encouraging my organization to come up with a useful product or service that no one has thought of before.

217. I encourage connections and communication between people and across departments within my company to foster new solutions.

218. To find a better way, I am looking at things from the perspective of people who disagree with me, who play "the fool," or who are on the "outside."

219. During the creative process I tolerate outrageousness, ambiguity, and even the chaos that will produce the most original ideas.

220. As a creative leader, rather than passively *accepting* change, I am *expecting* change.

221. Like a theater director, I see the big picture, but also pay attention to detail.

222. I have a vision of where I want to lead others.

223. I communicate my vision clearly, persuasively and with originality.

224. Like a visual artist, I see things that others do not see and am on the cutting edge.

225. Like a conductor leading a disciplined orchestra, I lead my team to work in harmony.

226. Like a writer, I know how to craft a message to make it memorable.

227. I have the motivation and discipline of an artist dedicated to her art.

228. I am imagining great opportunity where others see none.

229. I encourage risk-taking but not recklessness. Taking chances can sometimes lead to "failure," which we must learn from on our way to success.

230. I see the many alternative ways I can structure my organization.

231. I am delighted when everyone in a group interprets a creative challenge differently and produces an original variation.

232. I am so passionate about the vision that I am bringing all resources to bear to put it into action.

233. I fly in the face of convention. I take intuitive leaps of the imagination. Putting one foot after the other in logical fashion only takes me so far.

234. I doubt the obvious and challenge the accepted. In this way, I keep innovation alive.

235. I do not react to resistance defensively, but I work to gain understanding of the important creative changes being implemented.

236. I switch into different modes of thinking—analytical or intuitive—like I would switch into reverse gear if I drove into a blind alley.

237. I recognize and reward anyone who submits suggestions on how to improve ways of operating.

238. I am encouraging innovative ideas that lead to reduced expenditures and increased revenue.

239. To increase the chance of realization of a creative idea, I am budgeting for it and creating a timeline and benchmarks.

240. In creative leadership there is no room for the arrogant view that one has the only right way.

9

My Life is the Canvas Upon Which I Create

241. Creative thinking is important in all aspects of my life and is not the exclusive reserve of "artists" or any other small group.

242. I am creating with nature—planting a garden, arranging cut flowers or repotting plants.

243. I am painting or stenciling a design on a wall or simply admiring the colors and light that surround me.

244. I am gathering fresh ingredients, creating a culinary delight, and presenting it graciously on a colorful cloth with candles and flowers.

245. I am finding new combinations of textures, shapes and colors, and creating a striking new outfit, complete with accessories.

246. I am taking photographs to remember beautiful moments.

247. I do the reverse of what's expected. If what's expected is to take, I give; to argue, I agree; to resist, I bend; to be serious, I laugh.

248. If unable to avoid a dull activity, I make a game out of it, finding some novel way to liven it up.

249. I am writing down all the things I want to create in my life. I break the list down into specific projects I can accomplish by a target date.

250. I ask myself how I can improve things in everyday life, even if there is no obvious problem. This attitude leads to progress.

251. I am savoring a dish I rarely or never eat. I am slowly taking small bites to enliven every taste bud and am describing my experience.

252. I imagine what creative solution my favorite role model (living or dead) would propose to shed light on a problematical situation.

253. In the garden, I am smelling roses, lilacs, and hyacinths and remembering what all these delicious scents conjure up for me.

254. I have the capacity to make something out of next to nothing.

255. I am igniting imaginations and creativity is spreading like wildfire.

256. I don't "take" time for art, which cuts into my day, rather I "make" time, which adds fullness to my day.

257. Every choice I make involves a creative decision.

258. I shift as I perceive new developments on my horizon. As a creative person, I am extremely flexible in my responses.

259. I am letting go of attitudes, things, people, jobs, and situations that I have outgrown.

260. I realize that doing what I love brings good things to my life and those whose lives I touch.

261. A creative mind is uncluttered. I am clearing away the things of yesterday so I can make room for today.

262. I am gaining new insights about psychology at the mall, and on poetry at the beach.

263. Today I am doing one of my routines differently. I may travel a different route, rearrange my usual schedule, or change my menu.

264. To conjure up the warm emotion conducive to creativity, I am looking into the face of a baby, my best friend, or my dog.

265. I am trying new frames around old problems: Angular or curved? Ornate or simple? Traditional or modern? Adjustable or permanent?

266. I am focusing attention on the minute details of a mundane object in order to sharpen the observation skills out of which creativity is born.

267. I look through lenses that are clear enough for light to pass through and, for a change, choose glasses that are rosy-colored, dark, or tinged in ice-blue.

268. I embrace idiosyncrasies (my own and others') because they are the emblem of creative thinking and independent thought.

269. I am establishing boundaries for how much of my energy is spent on outward activities, and how much on inward creative pursuits.

270. After ingesting stimulating new information, I stop to reflect and integrate new ideas with former understandings.

10

I Practice the Art of Relationships

271. I always express my authentic self, whether alone or in relationship.

272. Like a wad of clay, my relationships can be fashioned into the shape I desire.

273. Through relationships with my loved ones, I discover myself and what's truly meaningful in life.

274. Just like each person is unique, each relationship is original and deserves the freedom to grow into its own form.

275. I am finding creative ways to relate to my family beyond our original family roles.

276. I do not always do what is expected when I encounter another person.

277. If I am in conflict, I listen carefully and share my point of view so we can find a creative resolution.

278. To people I care about I give thoughtful gifts that symbolize something I value about them.

279. I envision the good things I want for my loved ones and set about inspiring them to create the lives they want.

280. I create an ambiance with candles, music, and aromas when I want a romantic experience.

281. Friendships are fashioned like a sculpture over time by the care I am taking to keep in touch.

282. I create occasions to celebrate the wonderful people I know.

283. I am avoiding squeezing myself and my partner into roles conceived by others.

284. I use my creativity to open up new avenues for communication with people who may be shut down.

285. I am creative about determining the way of dividing labor and taking responsibility that is not based on gender.

286. I step back and look at a problem in a relationship from all different angles until a solution emerges.

287. In routines I rely on my own rhythms rather than roles.

288. I am creating the magnificence and miracle of love between two people.

289. I am imagining the deep understanding possible when each party brings his or her uniqueness to a relationship.

290. My lover's body is the canvas on which I am creating an array of sensations.

291. I celebrate the creation of a solid relationship in which I have exhibited as much patience and persistence as I do in making a work of art.

292. When a relationship comes to an impasse I pull out my inner compass and creative skills to map out a new direction.

293. Just as I study paintings by Rembrandt or Picasso, or listen to music by Mozart or The Beatles, I observe and tune into the moods of my beloved.

294. The pain and joy of my relationships are a source of material for my creative endeavors.

295. My love is the keyboard on which I play my most harmonious notes.

296. A child is as great a masterpiece as any work of art.

297. In creative problem solving, I honestly consider *my own role* in causing a problem—the solution may depend on *me* making an adjustment.

298. I recognize people who would derail me from my creative pursuits and know how to side step them.

299. I am guiding someone else on the creative path and am finding the relationship stimulates my own passion.

300. I support other creators. I do not envy, copy, or denigrate them.

11

My Passion is Unstoppable

301. I know big dreams may be the targets of ridicule and criticism. I dream big anyway.

302. In visualizing my dream, I imagine what it feels like, looks like, and sounds like. I picture where I am, who I'm with, and what I'm doing.

303. I am not waiting for a commission, a sabbatical, a grant, a studio. I am not waiting to be hired, "found," or recognized.

304. I am working now, on this day, with whatever I have at hand to create what fills my heart and mind.

305. I am not allowing anything to disturb my creative flow—phone, fax, or food; politics, people or pets.

306. If my work creates an uproar, like *The Dinner Party* by feminist Judy Chicago, I know that my ideas are having an impact!

307. I know that new ideas may seem strange to everyone at first, including me, and it may take time to find acceptance.

308. I stand by my own ideas, like Galileo, who did not retract his revolutionary theories of the solar system.

309. I am true to my own vision, as was Mary Cassatt, even though her parents did not want her to study with the Impressionists.

310. I am seeking truth as I see it, like Leonardo da Vinci did, even though he had to write backwards in his journals to protect himself from his critics.

311. I avoid people whose criticism stems from their ulterior motive of trying to make me fail.

312. I am grateful to people who offer constructive criticism with the purpose of helping me succeed.

313. If others laugh at my ideas I am not discouraged—their ridicule is a sure sign I am onto something significant.

314. I avoid mental prisons like perfectionism that impede my creativity.

315. I am daring to respond to my creative calling, even though it may not seem practical or initially financially rewarding.

316. I overcome roadblocks and pioneer alternate routes to my goals.

317. As my career evolves in an uneven way, I know the creative person's course is rarely straight and logical.

318. I believe that if I feel a deep desire, I may freely explore new directions and do not consider it dabbling.

319. I deflect criticism that my absorption in my work is selfish because I know the value it has for me and for those touched by it.

320. To the people who say my creative focus makes me self-centered I answer that if I am not the center of my own life, who is?

321. I will not put a clamp on my free creative spirit because of the jealousy and fears of others.

322. Nurturing one intimate relationship with a challenging art form is more meaningful than

juggling multiple shallow relationships with an admiring public.

323. I support and bond with other creative people in times when independent thinking is threatened. We do not ever stop speaking our truths.

324. I am finding like-minded people who understand my creativity, even if the public may mock me like the Impressionists were at first.

325. I am not daunted if people call my vision crazy. The best ideas start out on the mysterious fringe where lunatics, dreamers, and visionaries converge.

326. I understand, deep down, that my work has high value, knowing that creative people make important contributions to humankind.

327. The joy of creating is priceless to me whether I receive a monetary reward or not.

328. If my art attracts the attention of the world, I know that its true value lies not in the price tag but in how it moves the heart of someone else.

329. I celebrate every milestone, no matter how big or small, on my creative journey.

330. I enjoy creative exploration for its own sake, whether or not I reach a pre-determined "destination."

12

My Spirit Continually Renews Me

331. Whatever I create is the deepest expression of my own spirit.

332. I know that mind, body and spirit are connected and when I care for them, I am nurturing my creativity.

333. I am setting my priorities every day so that I leave more time for sacred creative pursuits and less for the mundane and trivial.

334. I am creating a sanctuary where I can easily go to remind myself of my creative purpose and joyful spirit.

335. I am enjoying a retreat for self-renewal of my creative energies through reflection, nature and the arts.

336. I am aware of the life force that animates me. I can connect to this force at any moment and find an infinite source of creative power.

337. Practicing my art form is a form of prayer.

338. When I stare myself down in the mirror I find the answer deep down about what I have to do to keep my creative spirit alive.

339. The forces that shape my art are much larger than I know.

340. Within me and within each of us lies valuable wisdom and extraordinary power.

341. Ultimately, the source of my creativity is not my mind fabricating ideas but the deep awareness of the life spirit within and without me.

342. I do not take credit as an individual for the source of my creativity.

343. I am passing on to the world the brilliance of the mystery that shines through me, but is not about me.

344. I am thrilled when, with a leap of imagination and faith, I am struck with an answer that I've been seeking.

345. I am feeling a sense of wonder and allowing the wonder to lead me to an astonishing breakthrough.

346. Like a potter, I am a partner in creation. The Higher Power creates the original clay, and the artist fashions the bowl.

347. The moment I enter a creative state of mind or start an endeavor, I feel larger forces shift to support me.

348. I am learning that when bad things happen they often lead to important lessons, insights, and stories that I use in my creative work.

349. I am transcending wounds by using them as a source of creative exploration.

350. I am dispelling anger because, although it can fuel creativity in the short-term, it won't lead to lasting works of high spiritual value and universal wisdom.

351. The adversity I have suffered has strengthened my character, made me more empathetic, and expanded my creative potential.

352. I am rewarded with such a deep sense of fulfillment from my art that consumption and competition are less appealing.

353. I want people whom I care about to know, though I create and change, that I am still the

same person who loves them and wants them in my life.

354. I have faith that what I am moved to create will mean something to someone somewhere, even if it's just one person.

355. My creative spirit protests against any form of rigidity.

356. I am dedicating resources—money, time and effort—to my creative garden, and I am seeing many flowers bloom.

357. My art is like the beautiful wild flowers on the side of the road unnoticed by the cars that rush past.

358. The act of creating and putting my creations into the world, even if no one else sees or hears them, is making the world a better place.

359. I shine my light as bright as it can be turned on—hiding my light does no one else any favor—it just keeps us all in the dark.

360. For someone with a creative mind, unanswered questions are more important than unquestioned answers.

I know that creativity is important

361. Creativity is one of the most important traits I can develop since it is crucial to thriving in our new century.

362. I am no longer holding on. I am letting go of the work I have created, just as a mother lets go of a grown child who is ready to find a place in the world.

363. I accept that all living beings pass away and I am using my time and insight to create something of value for the next generation.

364. I am not putting off to some future date the poem I can write, the picture I can paint, the song I can compose on this day.

365. I am a radiant being ready to shine my light in the world.

365 Daily Affirmations for Creativity

Now that you've come this far on your creative journey, rewrite your favorite affirmations from the previous 365 or create your own.

366. _____

367. _____

368. _____

369. _____

370. _____

Part 2

Exercises to Enhance

Creativity

365 Daily Affirmations for Creativity

FOR INDIVIDUALS

1. Clear the Screen of your Mind

One of the most important preparations for creativity is to still the mind. Take about fifteen minutes to sit comfortably in a chair. Hold your back upright to allow the energy to flow through your spine. Scan your body for any tension, and release it. Relax the muscles in your face, neck and shoulders, arms and hands. Be aware of your breathing. Relax your legs and feel your feet flat and firm on the ground.

Visualize that your mind is a computer, and wipe away all the distractions on the screen by pressing delete. Keep the screen clear. When thoughts start to intrude, as they will, let them float away and exit. When we are busy, our mind races and brain waves are measured as "beta." To reach the relaxed "alpha" state of mind perfect for creativity, practice this kind of meditation daily. It can be done before many of the following exercises or before you do your creative work.

2. Take a Deep Breath

To center yourself, keep focused on your natural breath, rising and falling. Sit with your spine straight in a chair and put your hands on your abdomen so you can feel the air naturally fill up your belly like a balloon when you breathe in, and deflate when you breathe out. Even a few minutes of this deep breathing will help calm you. If you focus on your breath for twenty minutes or more, you will begin to reach a state of heightened awareness ideal for creativity.

3. Laugh

Find something funny that will make you laugh. Collect this material so you can have access to it every day. It can be cartoons, funny films, stand-up comedian routines, pictures of animals, jokes, or funny stories that you share with friends. Make it a habit to see the humor in every situation. Humor is similar to creativity because both give us an unexpected lift.

Make other people laugh. In some Buddhist monasteries, if an initiate has a good belly laugh they are allowed time off from meditation because the laugh has the same desired effect on the spirit.

4. Visualize your Childhood

Often our earliest passions can be traced to our formative years. Meditate on a room in your childhood or youth where you did something creative. Imagine you are back there now. Do you hear or smell anything? What is it you like to do: play an instrument, make art, keep a diary, sew, or collect things? Do you most enjoy solitude or being with special people? What do you feel comfortable wearing? If there is something you can touch, what is it? How do you feel emotionally? Come back to the present and consider if these memories have anything to tell you about your deepest creative impulses.

5. Listen to Your Thoughts
Sit still in a quiet room for at least ten minutes. Observe with detachment what goes through your mind. Pay attention to the chatter; watch the endless stream of thoughts, ideas, and feelings and let them go. When negative or destructive thoughts arise, particularly judgmental ones, be alert. Often we allow judgmental thoughts to make us feel small and incompetent. Fears, doubts and regrets can get hold of you and shut down your creativity.

There are several ways to lessen the effect of negative thoughts. Literally picture yourself zapping them. Don't follow them or give them any credence; that only gives them power. Caroline Myss talks about unplugging from that negative power line and plugging into a positive energy source. Or if you can imagine your mind playing tapes, turn off the negative tape and throw it out. Get new positive tapes to play. Whatever method works for you, become aware of negative judgment and work on dispelling it, for it is the destroyer of creativity from the inside out.

6. Brag
When I was trained by Betsy Damon to lead No Limits for Women Artists sessions, she asked our group to brag about what we were most proud of. Most of us were uncomfortable doing that because it

sounded arrogant. We soon realized "bragging" is an important way to identify your strengths and true creative purpose. It's essential to knowing who you are.

7. List all the Activities You Enjoy

Make a list of all the things you can do excellently and effortlessly. Keep going, making the list as long as you can. This list is the key to your strengths and passions and what you're all about as a person. Now circle your favorite activities. When was the last time you did them? If you are putting them off or not making time for the things you enjoy, ask yourself why.

Your favorite activities indicate strengths that you need to develop, the things you need to do more of, the talents you need to bring to new levels, and the gifts you need to share with the world.

Look at your schedule and plan at least one hour in the next week to do a favorite activity.

8. Visualize Doors Opening

After meditation, deep breathing or centering, close your eyes and visualize yourself climbing down a ladder to a secret place where you can go to your private paradise.

On your path you reach a door that has been shut, closing you off from where you want to go. There's been a judgment either by your inner judge or by an assembly of outside critics that prevents you from entering here. Reject this judgment and reach out to open the door, using a magic phrase from childhood like, "Open sesame." The door opens out on to a clear day full of wondrous things you've been curious about since you were young.

Picture and sense everything about this desired paradise. It is where you express your truest and highest self. Here you are everything you were meant to be, and you are creating and giving to the world all your best gifts. Picture all the details of what you see. What are you doing? Who are you with? What are you wearing? What are you hearing, smelling, tasting, touching? How do you feel?

After you have absorbed the full sensory picture of your dream, begin on the path back. Climb the ladder back up, move your body, take a deep breath, and return refreshed to your creative work at hand.

9. Create a Picture of Your Dream

After doing the visualization above where you open the doors of your mind to your personal paradise, picture your marvelous creations as accomplished facts. Now make this mental picture concrete by creating it visually or describing it in writing. Preferably you will do both.

To create the picture visually, you may draw or paint it, or make a collage using many types of pictures from a variety of sources and art materials. Include a photograph of yourself in the collage. Use mixed media such as magazines, newspapers, drawings, designs, colored and textured papers, and objects such as ribbons, feathers, and shells. If you can picture it, you can make it happen. Post it where you can see it every day and be reminded of your dreams and goals.

To create a picture of your perfect paradise in writing, describe the picture in detail, using all the senses: sight, sound, taste, smell, and touch. Write the description of your creative success in such vivid, visual detail that upon reading it, pictures are created in the mind. Post it and review it daily. Henriette Anne Klauser wrote a book about how this process works called *Write it Down, Make it Happen.*

Your mind, which thinks in pictures, will absorb your vision as if it is real. Through the infinite power of the mind, you will start to make adjustments and attract into your life all that matches your vision. You will find that your dreams begin to take form in the real world.

10. Keep a Journal
Writing gets us in touch with our inner voice and helps us formulate our thoughts and feelings from which we create. Doris Lessing kept several notebooks, which she writes about in *The Golden Notebook.* Consider the following and determine which type of journal or combination of journals would work for you and make it a habit. What's important is that you write and write regularly.

Spill it on Paper
Write down all the thoughts floating around in your brain—fears, pains, frustrations, and angers—

anything you want. These pages are not necessarily meant for saving, but for eliminating thoughts that stop you from reaching a deeper state of mind. To further free yourself from negative thoughts, release them by ripping up the pages and discarding them. The cornerstone of Julia Cameron's program on developing creativity is to write three pages in longhand each day. She calls them "morning pages" and elaborates on this process in *The Artist's Way*.

Keep a Daily Diary
In this diary, write the day's events and any and all observations, ideas, dreams, feelings, desires, and plans.

Be Thankful
Sarah Ban Breathnach in *Simple Abundance* suggests you keep a special, beautiful gratitude journal in which you write everything you feel thankful for.

Take Notes on the Go
You may want another journal that is compact enough to carry with you. Sometimes you feel the need to write when you are away from home, your office, or if you lack a computer. Gather the loose sheets and place in a binder organized by date or topic.

Create an Illustrated Journal
I like to write in blank artist books with black or canvas covers that can be found in an art supply store. If you like, you can paint a design on the cover. Write

and sketch in this book, and paste in pictures that mean something to you—postcards, greeting cards, pictures and designs from magazines, newspapers or printed material from museums.

Record Your Dreams

Have a special book or pad by your bed so you can write down dreams as soon as you wake up. Dreams are your mind at work without the physical constraints of waking life. It can be the source of subconscious desires and understanding of precious vision. A dream is a voice so quiet that we have to work hard to tune into it, or it is drowned out by noises of everyday life or our own mind's chatter. Paying attention to dreams gives us practice in attending to our delicate inner life.

Here are some tips I learned from dream workers Anita Hall and Adair Heitmann when I was working on my novel about dreams. Write down as much as you remember from your dreams, even if it's just fragments. Give your dream a title. Describe objects in the dream as if you were talking to an alien. What are the qualities of the characters or objects of the dream? Who or what in your waking life has these qualities? What part of you is like that? What are your feelings in the dream? Are there any messages in the dream to help you understand or further your creativity? The more you pay attention to and write down your dreams, the more you will remember them.

11. The Combination Journal

What works for me is a combination of all the above journal ideas. Buy a thick binder and slip into the cover a beautiful illustration. Label the side with the year. Date and save all the bits of writing you do—on the computer, on a napkin in a restaurant, on a scrap piece of paper when traveling. Write only one kind of thing on a page; for instance a poem would have its own page, a list of gripes its own page, a design for a work of art another page. Do sketches and paintings on sheets of heavy art paper. Gather the sheets together, punch holes in them, or place in plastic sheets. Date them and place them in order in your binder. Use colored tabs if you'd like various sections, such as a chronological section and a section for thoughts on gratitude, dreams, specific creative project ideas and so on. Use a table of contents or index so you can easily refer to your ideas.

A two- or three-ring binder gives a creative person the most freedom to rearrange the pages, add and discard, and pull some out for other uses.

12. Organize Your Creative Ideas

It is essential that a creative person document and record the many thoughts and ideas that he or she generates. Choose a method of organization:

Build an Idea Bank

When you are working on a creative idea, keep a folder or binder that has plastic sleeves to organize and store special things that trigger creative thinking.

In here put postcards, pictures from magazines, articles, quotes, your sketches, diagrams, poems, compositions—references or raw material that are valuable resources for your project. Write your thoughts about how your concepts are evolving.

File Your Ideas in Folders
File ideas for creative projects in brightly colored file folders grouped in colorful hanging files. Keep an index. Review and purge regularly.

13. Plan Your "No Risk No Excuses" Goal

Imagine you are granted a wish. You have the power to bring to fruition a creative effort. Time and money are not considerations and you are guaranteed not to fail. What would you create? Draw a circle at the top of a page and write in the circle: My creative goal is _____.

Now write down ten reasons you have not yet achieved this goal. Write "But" in front of every reason. For instance, my creative goal is to give talks abroad about how to use art to open the spirit. *But* I don't know who can schedule me. *But* I don't want to be away from my family. Etc.

Now consider whether the items on your list are truly reasons, or merely excuses. Consider if your goal is merely a fantasy or something you will never work toward because you truly don't want to ever achieve this goal. That's all right. If, however, it is something you truly do want to pursue, study your list of "Buts" and determine if there are unconscious or irrational fears holding you back. Are you afraid of failing, not being competent, assuming debt, going public, losing your privacy, taking on too much, being too hectic, disturbing your life-style or relationships? Once you face the fears, you can work to overcome them. Lastly, consider the "Buts" on your list that you *can* do something about and begin by tackling each one. For instance, a solution for me is that I can take my family with me when I go away.

Now write down a creative goal that is authentic, post it in a prominent place, and work every day on dissolving blocks, and doing one thing that will bring you closer to achieving it.

14. Express Basic Emotion

This is a favorite drawing exercise that is an excellent way to identify and release emotions, and at the same time overcome a common block. Many people feel blocked by the false belief that they cannot make art if they cannot draw realistically. Yet abstract artists express emotion and ideas through simple line, color and shapes, which constitute a basic visual language accessible to everyone.

Hold a pencil ready, poised to make marks on a piece of scrap paper. Close your eyes and conjure up a memory of when you were terribly angry. Let that emotion fill you up and rise up through your arm and into your hand and pencil and spill out onto the page in scribbles. No need to draw an object, just let the anger come out in the lines.

Next take a deep breath in, and breathe out that negative emotion. As before, poise your pencil ready to scribble on another piece of paper. Now bring up a time when you felt like you were in paradise, when you were totally at peace, marvelously relaxed, in the perfect place at the perfect temperature, with people you love or enjoying solitude, doing what you love best, or doing nothing at all.

Let that feeling rise up and flow through your arm, hand, and pencil and onto the paper. What kind of lines are you making now? Compare the two scribbles. They are usually quite different. Others will readily identify the emotion behind them. Without drawing any particular object, you have succeeded in expressing an emotion. You may now experience less inhibition in using visual art, and feel more confident about your ability to communicate.

15. Meditate on a Mandala

"Mandala" means circle or center in Sanskrit. It is found in spiritual traditions in Asia, native cultures in North and South America, and in Judeo-Christian art and architecture. It is also found everywhere in nature. A mandala is a design that emanates from a center point, and involves cardinal points and symmetry. Meditate on a mandala to center yourself.

To create your own mandala, start with meditation to calm the mind. Play music—classical, baroque, jazz, or selections that relate to your current emotional state. Close your eyes and breathe and review your past; scan your body and feelings for the important things in your present, and picture what you want for the future. When you are ready, open your eyes and begin your mandala.

With pencil and paper (graph or blank), create your own design based on a circle, using balance and symmetry. You may employ a ruler and compass; or color with pencil, crayon or pastel. To end, meditate on the mandala you created. Does it give you any insight into your present state of mind?

16. Design Your Day Around Creativity

Observe and take note on how you feel as you go through a typical day. What are your rhythms? When do you feel most energized and creative? What activities or foods seem to dull you? Then make some changes. For instance, maybe reading the newspaper in the morning depresses your creative enthusiasm and would be best to do at another time of the day. Do the most inspiring and stimulating thing right before your designated time to create.

Carve out the time of day most conducive to creativity according to your own personal rhythms. Leave ample time in your day for activities that feed your creativity, which could be things like time with family and friends, correspondence, reading, music, and nature.

Stop living in your head at one point in every day. Take a break and enjoy the sensuality of grooming yourself. Cook something and enjoy the colors, textures, and smells of the food. Take a luxurious bath. Pet your animal. Garden. Listen to the birds.

Move your body every day. Put on your favorite dance music and work up a sweat. Take a class in yoga or martial arts. Or take a walk and while you are walking, look at the details of everything around you—people, nature, architecture—in a new way. Walking is the activity of choice for many creative people; it was a favorite of Thomas Jefferson.

17. Create Thought Pictures

Albert Einstein said he came upon his theory of relativity, which revolutionized the world of physics, by imagining himself riding on a light beam. He called his method of discovery "thought-pictures."

Through visualizing, the inventor Nikola Tesla came up with the alternating current dynamo and power transmission system that made the electric age possible. Visualize a problem by seeing or drawing it in simple graphic terms—symbols or stick figures will do.

18. Make Random Connections

To stimulate your thinking, consider a problem in relation to odd and random things you pick out from a magazine, the dictionary, or your immediate environment. For instance, ask yourself, how is this problem like "rain," "a bicycle," "a dog," or "cloning"? Connecting seemingly unrelated concepts may bring you sharp new insights.

19. Seek Ancient Wisdom
This fun exercise helps you connect with what you consider deep down to be true wisdom. With a particular problem or question in mind, find a picture book with Chinese characters, Arabic calligraphy, Hebrew writing or Egyptian hieroglyphics. Select one line. Ask your question. Now imagine that the inscription is the answer to your problem and you can translate what the ancient wisdom is telling you. Write it down and think about the "answer." This exercise will reveal what you intuitively understand about the solution.

20. Read Widely
Read biographies and autobiographies of the creative people you most admire. What routines did they establish for themselves? What was their creative process? When you are grappling with a creative problem, imagine how they would advise or guide you.

Read great literature. To produce new ideas, draw analogies. Compare a current problem to a poem or story and then see if any new solutions arise.

Read outside your field. What parallels can you draw between the challenges of creators in other disciplines and your own discipline? Was there a process used that led to a breakthrough that you can adapt?

Read or listen to the tapes of inspiring people who promote positive thinking and action.

Take a moment to read a poem, parable or a spiritual passage from various traditions. Then consider how the wisdom can guide you in your current situation.

21. Draw to Learn

If we study the ordinary long enough we uncover the extraordinary. Be like the draftsman who creates a line on a surface by imagining a little bug slowly crawling along the contours. Closely observe all the details of an object and you will find yourself in an alternative state of mind.

Leonardo da Vinci said he didn't learn to draw, he drew to learn. Choose an object or scene in nature to study closely for shapes, lines, tones, and colors. Note down what you observe. The result does not have to result in "art" but serves as a record of a genuine reflective state.

22. Activate your Creative Side

To activate the creativity of the so-called right brain, which controls the left side of your body, do the following:

- ♦ Scribble with your left hand.
- ♦ Breathe through your left nostril.
- ♦ Listen to music that conjures up memories.

- Do something with your hands—doodling, peeling a potato, and squeezing a ball. (Ninety-seven percent of the nerves in the hands are connected to the brain.)

23. Spend time with a Child

Spend an hour with a child to rediscover curiosity and wonder. You can make art, conduct an experiment, play a game, build a snowman, do a puzzle, read a story, bake bread, or decorate a dollhouse. Let the child take the lead.

24. Clear Out the Old

Clear out your old stuff in closets, drawers, and shelves. Throw out or give away clutter. Don't hang on to the old. Let go and make room for the new. Old familiar things had their use and served you well, but now they may be preventing you from growing. Appreciate them, then kiss them good-bye. This physical work of clearing out material objects has a spiritual dimension. Meditate on all the space you have created for new and wonderful things to come into your life.

25. Explore a Different Space

Go somewhere different to do creative work. Go to the beach, a mountain, lake, forest, or park. Or just take a bus ride to a new part of town and stop in at a local coffee shop. At the very least, go to a different room or sit in a different chair that has a different view. Write in your journal, sketch, or simply observe details in the new setting.

26. Expect the Muse to Show Up
Make an appointment with yourself to do your creative work. Determine how much time you can dedicate to your creativity every day. A friend who is a potter, Gay Schempp, says that everyone can find at least fifteen minutes—and once you get involved you usually work longer!

Create a space where you allow no one or nothing to interrupt or distract you. Set out the materials ahead of time and make your tools accessible. Clear off a working area. Show up, mind cleared, ready to work, and wait for the muse. You'll discover something: the muse is you. You are ready to create.

27. Plant Something
Participate in the miracle of nature's creations. Plant seeds or a bulb. Cultivate orchids. Cultivate an herb or vegetable garden. Place flowering plants around and engage in watering and fertilizing them. Understand the cycles of sowing and reaping and the connection with the blossoming of your own creative work.

28. Invite Feedback
Show your work to one or more trusted friends, advisors or mentors. Choose someone you respect. Ask for their genuine reaction. How does your work affect them? What do they like? Do they have any suggestions? Remember—suggestions are gifts that

will help you see your work objectively and may give you an idea on how to proceed. Of course, the final decision about your work always remains with you alone.

29. Take a Vacation

When you are burnt out is not the time to try to jump-start the imagination. Peaceful surroundings, sleep, and a complete break are needed to clear the mind and become renewed. Downtime is part of the creative process. The word solution comes from *solvere*, meaning to loosen. To arrive at solutions, you need to let go and lighten up.

Absorbing sights and sounds, smells, and tastes of a foreign culture gives you new perspectives and is always great stimulation for creativity.

30. Share your Gifts

Make a list of all the gifts that you can give to others. What energy, love, appreciation, wisdom, talents, or skills can you share that people need to have?

When you finish a creative project, thank all who contributed to it, celebrate your role in birthing it, and be joyous it has a life in the world beyond you.

What's the next creative idea pushing to be born?

•

Group exercises for trainers, seminar leaders, managers, or facilitators follow. However, you might also find that some or all of the suggestions will be useful for individuals as well.

GROUP EXERCISES

(For managers, trainers, facilitators, teachers and seminar leaders, to bring out creativity in classes, meetings, workshops and retreats)

1. Get 'Em Rollin'

If creativity is your aim, begin with something creative! Do something different, like recite a verse from a poem or song you love, read a favorite quote, or do something playful or humorous. Invite someone up to the front of the room who is good at telling jokes or doing a magic trick. A friend who's now a drummer, Randy Brody, used to begin his corporate team meetings by distributing little drums and spending a few minutes drumming. This was a primal way to release emotions and have the group "make music together." Team spirit went way up and their productivity regularly surpassed all other teams, baffling the supervisors who did not know their secret of the drum!

2. Ask Critical Questions

With a problem in mind, ask critical questions:
"What if?"
"Why not?"

"What next?
"Why?"
"What works?"
"What could work better?"

Innovators and comedians get a lot of material from asking:
"What's wrong with this picture?"

3. Remember Your Best Idea

Before you begin to work with a group, ask them to rate themselves on a scale of 1-10 regarding their own individual creative capacity. Then ask them to spend a few moments remembering being excited about a great idea they once had. Ask each to share with the group. They will gain a new appreciation of their own creativity and that of others. After this exercise, or after the class, session or course, ask the participants to rate themselves again. Usually the score goes way up!

4. Throw Out the "Junk"

To free the mind to grasp the new, at a team meeting set up a real or imaginary garbage container in the center into which all the "junk" is discarded. Toss out ideas and policies that are obsolete, inefficient and negative. A variation is to ask people to write down anonymously all the "gripes" they have about their day, the meeting, the team, anything they are feeling worried about or bothered by. With their permission you can read a few—they usually sound trite and funny. Then rip them all up and throw them away. This is the clearing away of blocks to the creative process.

5. Idea Streaming
Ask people to find a partner and then sit comfortably with heads facing in opposite directions but parallel and close enough to hear each other. Say, "Close your eyes and take a few deep breaths to relax. Observe the images that come to mind and then simply describe them out loud to your partner. Use the present tense and all five senses in your description." This is a technique developed by Win Wenger, which he uses as a free-form, spontaneous adventure in imagination, which has led to the development of numerous inventions and innovations.

6. Reward the Silliest or Dumbest Question
Before your group meets, ask them to write out as many questions they can think of about the project at hand—write ten, twenty, fifty questions! Remind them the only stupid question is the one not asked, and unanswered questions are better than unquestioned answers.

These questions will open up new avenues of exploration. Assumptions, which are unspoken and unconscious, often block progress. By questioning everything, assumptions get exposed and shattered. Have a mock competition for who can ask the dumbest or silliest question and award a dumb or silly prize.

7. Go On an Imaginary Journey

Living in human skin on the planet Earth, we are subject to many limitations. We have physical constraints of place, time, and money. However, our minds are free and unlimited. We can travel wherever we want. Ask your group to get comfortable, take a few breaths, close their eyes, and go with you on an imaginary journey.

You are going down a ladder to a kitchen or workspace. Pick up an everyday object. Watch yourself using it in an ordinary way. Now do something out of the ordinary with it.

As you walk along your path, you meet someone from the past who judged you, criticized you or blocked you. It could be an authority figure you were powerless to resist. See this person clearly in full detail. Remember how frustrated or angry you felt. Now speak up and talk back. You can share your true emotional reaction and what you think. Now tell the person to get out of your way, and move on.

You are again on your path. You see clearly where you're headed. Feel the joy of reaching your destination. Observe details closely and absorb with all your senses the paradise that surrounds you. When you are ready, slowly climb back up the ladder. Become aware of your breath again, move a part of your body, open your eyes and return refreshed to your waking life.

8. Combine Unlikely Elements

Some of the greatest innovations arise from simply combining two unlikely things. The printing press that revolutionized our civilization was simply a combination of the wine and the coin presses. When quantum physicists told us one hundred years ago that light could be *both* a wave and a particle, it changed our understanding of the universe.

Follow the example of artists who celebrated fantasy, the Dadaists and Surrealists, and design your own fantastic "juxtaposition." From magazines, cut out two images that are not usually connected and paste them down together. You may elaborate on your new image with drawing, color, or words. Discuss possible meanings of the new connection you created. These could be hilarious. Any ensuing laughter will prime your group for creativity.

9. Brainstorm or "White Board"

Choose an ordinary object, such as a piece of paper or an umbrella, and brainstorm all the various and possible uses of that object. Write them down on a white board. Quantity counts. The more ideas you generate, the more you move from ordinary to unusual ways of thinking. Sometimes groups generate hundreds of ideas that really make one think in extraordinary ways. For example, a piece of paper rolled up tight can be used to conduct an orchestra or prop up a hood.

Remember the rules of brainstorming:

- No judging, mocking, or excluding.
- Record every contribution.
- Relax and be outrageous; a silly idea can spark a great one.
- Piggyback on others' ideas—add, change, expand them.
- Have fun with this process!

10. Interpret an Image
Select pictures—photographs, reproductions, or original works of art—that will stimulate creative responses to the questions listed below. Project or display them one at a time so each is seen clearly by the whole group. Individuals may reflect and jot down responses. Pairs or small groups then discuss the following questions:

a. An image with two people, preferably a man and a woman. Ask: what would they be saying to each other? What is their relationship? What are they like? What makes you think that?

b. An image with some action. Ask: if this were a film, what happened in the previous scene? What will happen in the next scene?

c. An image of a landscape or cityscape. Ask people to enter the place with their imaginations and all their senses. What would it feel like being there? As they walk through, what would they hear, see, smell, touch or taste? Do they like being there?

Ask someone from each group to summarize their responses. Discuss which views are held in common and which interpretations vary greatly. We each have a wealth of private and individual experience to draw upon that makes each of us interpret things differently.

11. Observe and Describe

Observation is key to living deeply and successfully. It's a skill necessary to artists and writers but also to various roles from parent and scientist to salesperson and negotiator. Studying images develops this essential skill. Distribute to each person a postcard, an 8 x 10-inch photograph, or a large image from magazines. Ask each person to observe the image carefully, and spend ten minutes writing a detailed description of the image. Then ask them to exchange their descriptions with a partner. The partner is to draw what they imagine from the description. Discuss how close the drawing is to the original image. This exercise also gives feedback on clarity of communication.

12. Ask Everyone to Play in the Relay

Let your group or team know that each person plays an important role in the innovative process, which is like a relay game. Innovation is not the sole province of those usually recognized as "creative" because they generate many ideas. This person often is the one who starts off the process. Then, from the mountain of ideas generated, a second person is needed to select the workable ideas to be advanced. A third person's role is to refine the ideas through challenging them further and assigning specific measurements, such as cost, size, and time. Finally, the best idea needs to be implemented, which takes someone with executive skills. There are tools that can help assess who is best at each of these roles and how the team can work well together to produce innovations.

Attend a concert, play, or dance performance together and observe how the symphony, band or troupe must work together as a team in order to achieve excellence.

13. Make a Switch
Ask two people to switch responsibilities and then meet to compare notes on how responsibilities could be carried out differently.

Or switch something in the surroundings. Ask people to change something in their environment—a picture, a plant, a screen saver—that makes their space different. Ask them to observe whether their approach to work changed in some way as well.

14. Minimize the Problem
Sometimes we are overwhelmed and don't know where to begin to work on a situation. Tell yourself

it's "no big deal." This reduces the burden, magnitude, and tension. Once you minimize the problem, you can simplify it so you see the essentials and can take action. Begin with one small step.

15. Ask for Input
In the class or group, ask a person to present a problem and enlist the support of others in solving it—they may offer suggestions or approaches. In a variation, a person describes his or her creative idea and the group pictures it and affirms it.

16. Share Silently
Ask each person to write in the center of a large sheet of paper (flip chart sized) a challenge he or she is facing, or a creative idea. Post the sheets on the walls or lay them on tables, so that the group can circulate silently and read them and add their input by writing on the sheets.

If it's a creative idea, individuals can add to the idea, alter it, find flaws, or sing praises. All written comments can trigger reactions; you can piggyback on others' ideas. You can use different colored pens or Post-it® notes. For instance, use blue to add to an idea, orange to alter or find a flaw, and purple to praise it.

17. Create A Group Success Collage or "Dream Board"
With images of success in their minds, ask group members to create a large collage with pictures they draw or cut out of magazines or newspapers or from

any printed material from the group. Glue down the images (acrylic media works) and embellish the collage with simple materials like pencils, markers, and pastels. You may add words, but make the images the primary part of the collage.

We are surrounded by words in our daily work life and they are usually logical in nature. Making any image at all—symbols, stick figures, colors, shapes and lines—brings out from us our intuitive, creative, emotional, and spiritual understandings. Artistic quality is not the point. The aim is to access functions of the brain that are rarely used but important for seeing the whole picture.

Post the group collage where all can see it daily. The mind and spirit will begin to make adjustments that will work toward making the dream a reality. You will be amazed at how many of the outcomes portrayed in the images will be implemented.

18. Break Down a Problem
Take a problem, preferably one that is current and important. Ask people to define it in a few sentences. Now ask them to identify the specific parts of the problem, and draw symbols of those parts on separate pieces of paper. Lastly, discuss how to solve each separate part, rearrange the parts, and see if a new solution emerges.

19. Take a Nature Walk
No, it's not just for kindergarten. People of all ages will benefit from being out in nature and observing

beautiful details. The famous acting teacher, Stanislavski, recommended noticing the beauty of nature as a way of stimulating creativity.

A break to enjoy nature can refresh the most listless meeting. Ask people to be silent and carefully observe details—shapes and colors and textures. When you return ask people to reflect or write a short description or haiku poem. They may share if they like.

20. Research Creative People
Ask each person to research the biography of a great thinker or creator such as Leonardo da Vinci, Darwin, Picasso, Einstein, Jefferson, Mozart, Margaret Mead, Shakespeare, Eleanor Roosevelt, Abigail Adams, Gandhi or Gershwin. Each person is to bring to the group a habit or attitude of that person and conjecture how it relates to the creative project at hand.

21. Play with a Problem
Have fun with an abstract problem by giving it a concrete shape. Allow your mind to move up, down and all around it. Imagine what would happen if elements were increased or decreased. For example, if you are having a problem finishing a creative project, you could increase the time you allot for it, and decrease the interruptions and distracting noises. Now take the problem and slowly, in turn, consider what would happen to its shape if you stretch it, divide it, repeat it, revolve it, reverse it, or distort it. You just

may wind up with something outlandish enough to be original.

22. Ask "The Fool"

The Fool of the Court was valued for giving the King the truth disguised as jest. Making fun of a plan can lead to discovery of crucial flaws. If you can't find a solution, maybe you are too enmeshed in its complexities and could use the refreshing view of an "Outsider." Try the following role-play.

One person is to play the role of an Outsider—a foreigner or alien from outer space. Another person is to play the Insider and try to explain the problem in detail and as simply as possible. The Outsider can ask questions, and ask for explanations and definitions. The Insider attempts to redefine the problem using totally new words and fresh phrases. The Insider can make no assumptions that the Outsider understands anything. The group is to observe closely, writing down bits of the dialogue (or tape it). Discuss insights that come up. What you find out may surprise you.

23. Take a Cosmic Perspective

To generate a sense of wonder, observe the stars, study astronomy, look at images of far away galaxies, and consider the staggering distances. Provide black paper, colored chalk, pastel or paint and ask people to express some of the awe at the marvels and magnitude of the universe. Create explosions, nebulae, orbiting planets and comets, black holes, red giants, white dwarfs, and spiral galaxies. This exercise helps us see the big picture, gain perspective, and feel genuine awe, all of which lead to opening minds.

24. Create a Tribal Culture

You may prepare this by displaying pictures from an ancient or exotic culture or a depiction of a place from science fiction. Talk about all the elements that make up a culture. Divide the group into two; each group is to create their own culture. Give each the starting point of a climate and environment, for instance, an isolated tropical island, or a high mountain.

The group is to come up with a name for their "tribe" after they invent all the following aspects of culture:

- Foods they eat
- Religious or spiritual beliefs, values and morals
- A saying they go by
- Any customs or rituals, such as birth, coming of age, mating, marriage, death
- Language and other means of communication
- Clothing and style
- Art and architecture
- Music they play
- Work they do and products they make
- Laws, rules, rewards and punishments
- Fun and sports

Each group writes down the culture of the tribe, or constructs a model of a town, artifacts, clothing, or anything that represents the culture visually with art materials such as pencils, markers or paint, cut construction paper, cardboard, scissors and tape.

Ask the two groups to explain their culture to each other. Now tell them that the two cultures will encounter each other. What will the experience be? Is there aggression and obliteration of the other culture? Or integration and tolerance? Do the two cultures "merge" (like corporations)? Imagine what happens. Discuss insights gained that relate to contemporary culture in the workplace, or current events and cultural conflicts.

25. Describe a Group's Culture

Every group has a culture, whether it's a board, organization, club, company, house of worship, school or family. Using the elements of culture listed above, do the following exercises:

Step One. Describe the actual culture of the group. For example, around food: what kind of food is served in the cafeteria? Where do people have lunch and what do they eat and how long are the breaks? Is food brought in when people work late? Around values: what is the vision and mission? How do people communicate? Is there a dress code? Which behaviors lead to rewards?

Step Two. Now describe the ideal group culture that is most desirable.

Step Three. Discuss the differences between the actual and ideal description.

Step Four. What changes can be made in the present culture to make it more like the ideal culture? Make a plan to start with one simple thing.

Optional. Create visuals of the actual and ideal culture, either with collage, symbols and stick figures, or abstractly with line, shape and color.

26. Separate Components that Act Like Children
Imagine that the incongruent components of a problem are like arguing children. Ask people in the group to role-play children who need a change in position. Split them far apart. Assign attributes of the problem to each child. Ask the children what their demands are. Ask observers if they gain any clarity seeing the parts of the problem individually.

Next, seat the "problem children" very close together. Now that they're pressed to find a way to settle their differences, ask them and the observers if they see any resolution to ways they can work or play together.

27. Go on A Weekend Retreat
Gather your most creative friends and colleagues to pick their brains. Ideally go to a safe and restful spot

to spend the weekend. Brainstorm and stay up as late as you like. Arise early enough to watch the sun rise. Brainstorm, meditate, walk, laugh, play, write, and create images all day long. You will find you arrive at a different state of mind. Consider if there is anyone in this group that you would want to collaborate with in the future.

28. Visualize A Happy Ending on a Big Screen

Ask the group to imagine they are in a movie theatre with a big movie screen, like the IMAX oversized screens, before the show begins. They may let go, relax, and sit upright with hands free and legs firmly on the ground. Ask them to close their eyes, and pay attention to their breathing by observing it as they would the ocean. One cannot change the ocean, but one can watch the waves come in and go out. In the same way, just be aware of inhalation and exhalation. Ask them to imagine the mind like a giant movie theatre. Think BIG.

To demonstrate that everyone can visualize, ask the group to close their eyes and imagine projecting onto the big screen three different scenes in succession. Imagine an open field of waving green grass; then switch to a dark blue sky over a stormy sea; then project a wide expanse of golden desert.

Now ask them to visualize on the giant screen a film about the project the team is working on. Visualize a happy ending, a positive outcome. What would success look like, taste like, smell like, and sound like? Who are the people enjoying the success? What does it feel like emotionally?

After they open their eyes and the movie is over, ask them to verbalize what they saw in their minds' eye.

29. Create a Team Cheer

Encourage the group to expect victory and see themselves triumphant and celebrating! Ask participants to buy into the goal by describing vividly all the results and concrete things that will happen when they succeed. Then ask each one to write a cheer for the group to get them pumped up. Work on creating one for the group. For example, "We are the best at _____!" Fill in the blanks, include specific and concrete details, and post the statement for all to see.

When the group does achieve a victory, make sure to celebrate!

30. Design a Creativity Lab

To help promote creativity, ask the group to design for themselves an inspiring group space in which creativity is fostered. Bring in comfortable furniture, flowers and plants and stimulating art works. Play classical or baroque music, and put up boards or flip charts with lots of colored pens around to jot down ideas.

Add the element of water, which is soothing and is known to stimulate creativity. It could be a fountain, a fish tank, a view out the window, a beautiful painting or photograph of a sea or lake. Play a tape with sounds of nature—a waterfall, rain in a forest, or the sound of the ebb and flow of surf and waves crashing on the shore.

Set up a small refrigerator and stock it with healthful snacks. Have some toys, games, puzzles, brainteasers, picture books, and art materials available on shelves. Keep tables uncluttered. Encourage people to meet in this space to informally discuss or play with ideas so the creative adventure continues.

Part 3

Resources

BOOKS AND ARTICLES

Angelou, Maya. *I Know Why the Caged Bird Sings.* New York: Random House, 1969.

Ayres, Joe; Hsu, Chia-Fang; Sawant, D. Darshan; Silva, John; Story, Traci; Wongprasert, Tanichya K. "Effects of performance visualization on employment interviews." *Communication Quarterly*, Spring 2001, v49 i2, pp. 160–171.

Baum, Kenneth with Richard Turbo. *The Mental Edge: Maximize Your Sports Potential with the Mind-Body Connection.* New York: Penguin Putnam, Inc., 1999.

Best, Dennis. "Visualization: the mental road to accomplishment." *Coach and Athletic Director,* August 1999, vol. 69, pp. 44-46.

Borysenko, Joan. *Inner Peace for Busy People: 52 Simple Strategies for Transforming Your Life.* Carlsbad, CA: Hay House Inc., 2001.

Boorstein, Daniel J. *The Creators: A History of Heroes of the Imagination.* New York: Random House, 1992.

Breathnach, Sarah Ban. *Simple Abundance: A Daybook of Comfort and Joy.* New York: Warner Books, 1995.

Buckingham, Marcus and Clifton, Donald. *Now, Discover Your Strengths: How to Develop Your Talents and Those of the People You Manage.* New York: Simon & Schuster, Inc., 2002.

Cameron, Julia. *The Artist's Way: A Spiritual Path to Higher Creativity.* New York: Penguin Putnam, 1995.

_____. *Walking in This World: The Practical Art of Creativity.* New York: Penguin Putnam, 2002.

Canfield, Jack and Mark Victor Hansen. *Chicken Soup for the Soul®.* Deerfield Beach, FL: Health Communications, 1993.

Canfield, Jack; Mark Victor Hansen, and Les Hewitt. *The Power of Focus: How to Hit Your Business, Personal and Financial Targets with Absolute Certainty.* Deerfield Beach, FL: Health Communications, 2000.

Canfield, Jack, Bruce Jenner, Janet Luongo, Brian Tracy, et. al. *Mission Possible!* Volume Four. Sevierville, TN: Insight Publishing Company, 2002.

Canfield, Jack and Janet Switzer. *The Success Principles: How to Get From Where You Are to Where You Want to Be.* New York: HarperResource, 2005.

Chicago, Judy. *The Dinner Party: A Symbol of Our Heritage.* Garden City, NY: Anchor Press/Doubleday, 1979.

Cifuentes, Lauren and Hsieh, Yi-Chuan Jane. "Visualization for middle school students' engagement in science learning." *Journal of Computers in Mathematics and Science Teaching,* Summer 2004, v23 i2, p. 109 (29).

Clarke-Epstein, Chris. *78 Important Questions Every Leader Should Ask and Answer.* New York: AMACOM, 2002.

Danzig, Bob. *There is Only One You.* New York: Child Welfare League of America, 2003.

deBono, Dr. Edward. *Lateral Thinking: Creativity Step by Step.* New York: Harper & Row, 1970.

Easwaran, Eknath. *Meditation: A Simple 8-point Program for Translating Spiritual Ideals into Daily Life.* Tomales, CA: The Blue Mountain Center of Meditation, 1991.

Gardner, Howard. *Creating Minds: An Anatomy of Creativity Seen Through the Lives of Freud, Einstein, Picasso, Stravinsky, Eliot, Graham, and Gandhi.* New York: Basic Books, 1993.

Gawain, Shakti. *Creative Visualization: Use the Power of Your Imagination to Create What You Want in Your Life*. Novato, CA: New World Library, 2002.

Gelb, Michael J. *How to Think like Leonardo da Vinci: Seven Steps to Genius Every Day*. New York: Dell, 2000.

Gimbutas, Marija. *The Language of the Goddess*. San Francisco: Harper & Row, 1989.

Hall, Anita. *The Stars at Night*. Philadelphia, PA: Xlibris Corporation, 2002.

High, Jana L. and Marilyn Sprague-Smith with Janet Luongo, et. al. *The Princess Principle: Women Helping Women Discover Their Royal Spirit*. Dallas, TX: R&W Publishers, 2003.

Kemp, Michael. "Visualization works in reaching business goals." *American Salesman,* May 2000, v. 45, p. 18.

Klauser, Henriette Anne. *Write It Down, Make It Happen: Knowing What You Want–and Getting It!* New York: Simon & Schuster, Inc., 2000.

Kundtz, David. *Stopping: How to Be Still When You Have to Keep Going*. Berkeley, CA: Conari Press, 1998.

Langrehr, John. *Teaching our Children to Think.* Bloomington, IN: National Educational Service, 2001.

Lapp, Janet. *Dancing with Tigers.* Rancho Santa Fe, CA: Demeter Press, 2004.

_____. *Positive Spin.* Rancho Santa Fe, CA: Demeter Press, 1994.

Lessing, Doris. *The Golden Notebook.* New York: HarperCollins, 1962, 1999.

Levesque, Lynn C. *Breakthrough Creativity: Achieving Top Performance Using the Eight Creative Talents.* Palo Alto, CA: Davies-Black Publishing, 2001.

Licauco, Jaime T. "How Visualization Improves Physical Performance." *Asia Africa Intelligence Wire,* May 27, 2003.

Magrath, Jane. "Polyphony: Visualization and music study," *American Music Teacher,* December/January 2003-2004, p. 48 (3).

McGraw, Phillip C. *Self Matters: Creating Your Life from the Inside Out.* New York: Simon & Schuster, Inc., 2001.

McMeekin, Gail. *The 12 Secrets of Highly Creative Women.* New York: MJF Books, 2000.

Michalko, Michael. *Thinkertoys: A Handbook of Business Creativity for the 90s*. Berkeley, CA: Ten Speed Press, 1991.

Myss, Caroline. *Sacred Contracts: Awakening Your Divine Potential*. New York: Three Rivers Press, 2001.

_____*Invisible Acts of Power*. New York: Simon & Schuster, Inc., 2004.

Peters, Tom. *The Circle of Innovation: You Can't Shrink Your Way to Greatness*. New York: Vintage Books, 1997.

Rowland, Elizabeth and Molotsky, Leonard. *Resource of Creative and Inventive Activities*. Richardson, TX, National Inventive Thinking Association, 1994.

Ray, Michael and Myers, Rochelle. *Creativity in Business: Based on the Famed Stanford University Course That Has Revolutionized the Art of Success*. New York: Doubleday, 1986.

Reeve, Christopher. *Nothing is Impossible: Reflections on a New Life*. New York: Random House, 2004.

Robbins, Anthony. *Unlimited Power: The New Science of Personal Achievement.* New York: Simon and Schuster, Inc., 1997. Audio book, 2000.

Root-Bernstein, Robert and Michele. *Sparks of Genius: The Thirteen Thinking Tools of the World's Most Creative People.* New York: Houghton Mifflin Co., 1999.

Samuels, Mike and Samuels, Nancy. *Seeing with the Mind's Eye.* New York: Random House Inc., 1975.

SARK. *Make Your Creative Dreams Real.* New York: Fireside, 2004.

Scott, Phil. "The Mind of a Champion." *Natural Health*, Jan-Feb 1997 v. 27, n.1, pp. 98-102.

Tolle, Eckhart. *The Power of Now: A Guide to Spiritual Enlightenment.* Novato, CA: New World Library, 1999.

Van Oech, Roger. *A Whack on the Side of the Head* (revised edition). New York: Warner Books, 1990.

Wacker, Watts and Taylor, Jim. *The Visionary's Handbook.* New York: HarperCollins, 2000.

Yager, Jan. *Effective Business and Nonfiction Writing.* Second edition. Stamford, CT: Hannacroix Creek Books, Inc., 2001.

_____. *365 Daily Affirmations for Creative Weight Management.* Stamford, CT: Hannacroix Creek Books, Inc., 2002.

Zander, Rosamund Stone and Zander, Benjamin. *The Art of Possibility: Transforming Professional and Personal Life.* Boston, MA: Harvard Business School Press, 2000.

WEBSITES*

www.openminds-opendoors.com Janet Luongo's resources and articles on creative leadership skills: vision, innovative teams, diversity, and the art of peaceful persuasion.

www.awakeningartistry.com The Art of Living Your Dreams website features Tama J. Kieves, a "Harvard lawyer who left it all to have it all." Tama is author of *This Time I Dance: Trusting the Journey of Creating the Work You Love.*

www.creativityforlife.com A guide to living your life creatively.

www.creativityworkshop.com Creativity creative writing, drawing, storytelling and personal memoir.

www.howdesign.com Find the article by George Shaw, "Your Creative Life: The Proof is in the Process." Many interesting links.

---

*Because website addresses or even their existence on the Internet may change at any time, neither the author nor the publisher can guarantee the accuracy of any of these listings.

www.jackcanfield.com Jack Canfield, co-author of *Chicken Soup for the Soul®* best-selling book series, offers speeches, workshops, tele-seminars, books and tapes that help people live fully and successfully.

www.mindtools.com A rich site to help you understand the essential skills and techniques to help you to excel in your career, whatever your profession.

www.planetsark.com SARK, an artist featured on the PBS series, Women of Wisdom and Power, is the author of *Make Your Creative Dreams Real*.

www.spiralmuse.com A place where any woman can contribute her artwork, essays, poetry, visions for the world, events and products, etc. Resources on community, activism, art and the spirit.

www.winwenger.com Win Wenger offers techniques to increase the powers of the mind.

www.womenscreativity.com For creative women. Showcases a visual arts gallery, inspiring articles, books and e-books on creativity, and a free email newsletter.

ASSOCIATIONS*

www.getty.edu/artsednet/ ArtsEdNet offers a wealth of information on the arts and education from the Getty Center.

www.creativeeducationfoundation.org Creative Education Foundation presents the oldest and largest creative event in the world, the Creative Problem Solving Institute.

www.invention-ifia.ch/ International Federation of Inventors Associations is a non-profit non-governmental organization with members in 90 countries that seeks to improve the status of inventors and promote cooperation.

www.iwwg.com International Women's Writing Guild is a network for the empowerment of women through writing.

---

*Because associations may change their names, merge with another association, or even go out of existence, website addresses or even their existence on the Internet may change at any time, neither the author nor the publisher can guarantee the accuracy of any of these listings.

www.menc.org National Association for Music Education encourages the study and making of music by all.

www.naww.org National Association of Women Writers is a non-profit where women unite to write.

www.aahperd.org/nda National Dance Association aims to increase knowledge, improve skills and encourage sound professional practice in dance education.

www.americanpenwomen.org National League of American Pen Women promotes the development of creative talent of professional women in the arts.

www.nationalwriters.com National Writers Association provides a community of writers and friends where "Great Works begin."

www.uua.org Unitarian Universalist Association is a liberal religious organization.

www.nationalwca.com Women's Caucus for Art is a non-profit organization that promotes and supports equal opportunity and visibility for women's art.

About the Author

Janet Luongo, an artist and writer, gives speeches and workshops to develop the qualities leaders need that artists have mastered: vision, creative thinking, and power in communication. President of Open Minds Open Doors (www.openminds-opendoors.com), she works internationally with associations, educational, and non-profit organizations to develop creative ability and innovative teams.

She exhibits regularly in the New York Metropolitan area with the Women's Caucus for Art-Connecticut, a non-profit association she founded in 1990 that helps women artists gain visibility. She exhibited in New York, Paris, and Geneva, when she lived in Switzerland for eight years, teaching art at the International School. As an award-winning vice-president of The Discovery Museum, she produced five TV documentaries on innovative multicultural programs.

Janet is published in two anthologies: *Mission Possible Volume 4* and *The Princess Principle: Women Helping Women Discover Their Royal Spirit.*

She serves the National Speakers Association as chair of the educators expert group and as past chapter president. An adjunct professor of communication at Sacred Heart University, Janet has a master's degree in education and resides in Connecticut with her husband who directs high school plays. Their grown son is an artist, athlete, and a creative problem-solver in mathematics.